Reflect on the precepts of the Lord, let His commandments be your constant meditation; then He will enlighten your mind, and the wisdom you desire He will grant.

Sirach 6:37

The intent and
purpose of this volume is to
give you faith, hope and inspiration.
Hopefully it will help bring peace and
tranquility into your life. May it be a
reminder of God's love, guidance
and His many blessings.

Our publications help to support our work
for needy children in over 130 countries
around the world. Through our programs,
thousands of children are fed, clothed,
educated, sheltered and given
the opportunity to live
decent lives.

Salesian Missions wishes to extend special thanks and gratitude to our generous poet friends and to the publishers who have given us permission to reprint material included in this book. Every effort has been made to give proper acknowledgments. Any omissions or errors are deeply regretted, and the publisher, upon notification, will be pleased to make the necessary corrections in subsequent editions.

First Edition Printed in the U.S.A. by Concord Litho Group, Concord, NH 03301.

Reflect Upon Your Blessings

from the
Salesian Collection

Compiled and Edited
by Jennifer Grimaldi

Illustrated by
Russell Bushée, Paul Scully,
Robert Van Steinburg, Bob Panteleone,
Dorian Lee Remine, Frank Massa
and Maureen McCarthy

Contents

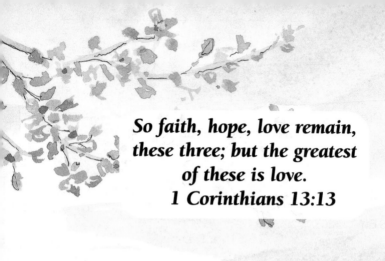

So faith, hope, love remain, these three; but the greatest of these is love.
1 Corinthians 13:13

Happy Are We

Happy are we who walk in His ways
And follow in His footsteps day by day.
Sharing our love with one another
And lightening the burdens of our brothers.

Our souls are lifted and filled with delight
As we dwell on Nature's glorious sights.
Wonders and beauty beyond compare
Created for us by a God who cares.

Happy are we when with God we are filled
And always try endlessly to fulfill His will.
Precious are we in His holy sight,
Know He remains with us day and night.

Happy are we as we walk life's highway
Spreading joy and happiness each day.
May we never wander far from the fold
And always be His to have and to hold.

Shirley Hile Powell

*I look for Your salvation,
Lord, and I fulfill Your
commands.*
Psalm 119:166

7

...To You, Lord, I call; my Rock, do not be deaf to me... Psalm 28:1

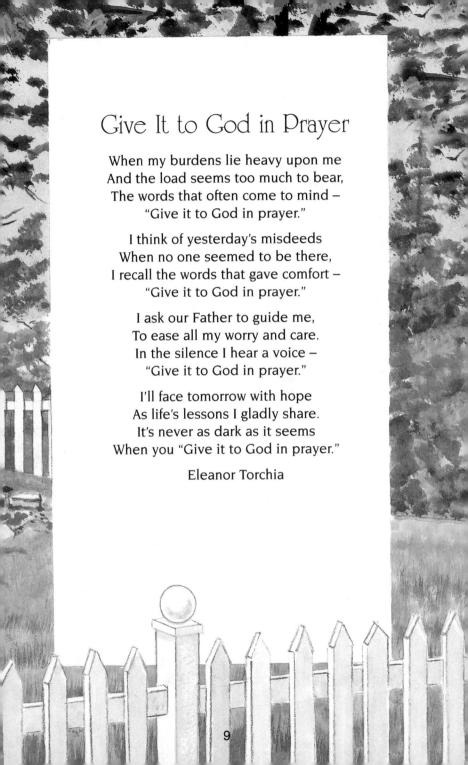

Give It to God in Prayer

When my burdens lie heavy upon me
And the load seems too much to bear,
The words that often come to mind –
"Give it to God in prayer."

I think of yesterday's misdeeds
When no one seemed to be there,
I recall the words that gave comfort –
"Give it to God in prayer."

I ask our Father to guide me,
To ease all my worry and care.
In the silence I hear a voice –
"Give it to God in prayer."

I'll face tomorrow with hope
As life's lessons I gladly share.
It's never as dark as it seems
When you "Give it to God in prayer."

Eleanor Torchia

Love Shared

Love shared is a sweet adventure
That can last our whole lives through;
Seeing us past the hard times,
Making hopes and dreams come true.
Love shared enhances blessings
That are sent from God above,
And we assure a bright tomorrow
As we fill each day with love.

Catherine Janssen Irwin

Beautiful Days

Each day is very beautiful,
I know this to be true.
No matter where we are in life,
Beauty is there, too.

The sun that rises in the sky
Is always beautiful to see,
And how gorgeous is another's smile
That is meant for you and me.

Music, paintings, buildings, too,
The flowers in a vase,
There is so much in our world
That shows God's beauty and His grace.

Barbara Joan Million

Fill us at daybreak with
Your love, that all our days
we may sing for joy.
Psalm 90:14

If you come with us, we will share with you the prosperity the Lord will bestow on us.
Numbers 10:32

A Traveler's Prayer

Whenever I travel
By land or by sea,
I always invite God
To travel with me.
For He is the One
Who created it all…
The tiniest star,
Each mountain so tall.
This is the One
With whom I would share
Each traveling moment,
Each traveling prayer.
And when I come home,
I look back and say,
Thank You, dear God,
For blessings each day!

Margaret Peterson

Gift

For God so loved
The world He gave
His only Son
Our souls to save.
Pause now, dear ones.
Let us reflect
Upon the Christ;
Pay Him respect.
Quiet ourselves
To quell the din
Of daily stress;
Invite Him in.
Open the chambers
Of our hearts,
Receive the love
He will impart.
Pause and accept
His gift… release
Ourselves to know
His inner peace.
For God so loved,
He gave His Son
To give His peace
And joy, dear one.

Anna Lee Edwards McAlpin

Yellow Butterfly

Dainty, yellow butterfly,
On fragile wings you flutter by.
Here awhile, then out of sight.
Oh, but you bring such delight
To the eyes that follow you,
As you seek sweet drops of dew
From the flowers white and red,
Planted in my garden bed.
Dainty, yellow butterfly,
Merrily you flutter by.
Yours are all the meadows fair,
Yours a season without care.
God provides the nectar sweet
For your daily, pleasing treat.
Frolic in the sun's warm rays
All your transitory days.

Regina Wiencek

*I will delight and rejoice in
You; I will sing hymns to
Your name, Most High.*
Psalm 9:3

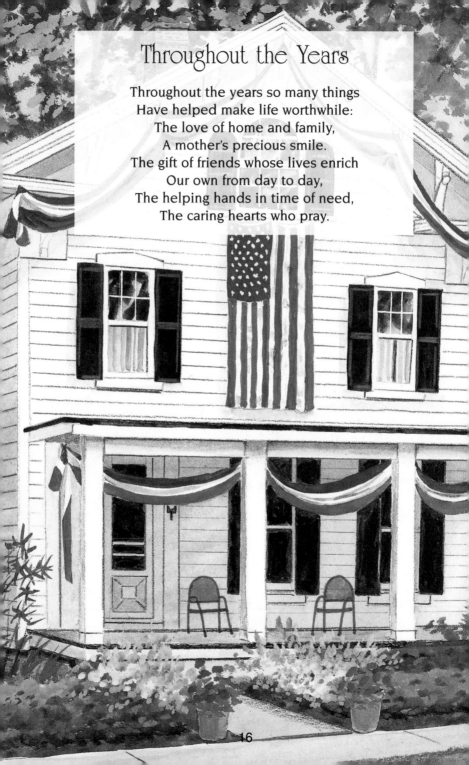

Throughout the Years

Throughout the years so many things
Have helped make life worthwhile:
The love of home and family,
A mother's precious smile.
The gift of friends whose lives enrich
Our own from day to day,
The helping hands in time of need,
The caring hearts who pray.

The beauties of God's wondrous world
Around us everywhere,
The songs of birds, the sunshine's gold,
The flowers bright and fair.
The strength to do our daily tasks,
The times of laughter, too,
The wealth of mem'ries we have stored,
The dreams we've seen come true.
The gift of music, favorite books,
So much make life worthwhile –
The special joy that children bring,
Each hug and happy smile.
The worship place where peace is found,
The knowledge of God's love,
The faith that's kept us through the years,
His guidance from above.
For these, and countless other gifts
How grateful we should be.
Oh, may we somehow find the way
To live more thankfully.

Beverly J. Anderson

Praise Him by the Hour

Oh, praise Him by the hour!
Yes, glorify His name
In the warmth of the sun
Or in the cool of rain.
Praise Him! Never ceasing!
On us He won't give up;
He wipes away each tear
And overflows our cup.

Steven Michael Schumacher

Cast Not a Stone...

Cast not the first stone, my friend,
When someone goes astray;
When a brother slips and falls,
Lift him up, instead, and pray.

Pass not along the sordid news
Of someone's sin displayed;
Lift him up and help him stand
Because for him you've prayed.

Kay Hoffman

*I trust in Your faithfulness. Grant
my heart joy in Your help, that I
may sing of the Lord, "How good
our God has been to me!"*
Psalm 13:6

At God's Command

The panoramic change of time
As seasons come and go,
Speaks simply of His wondrous love
As if displayed to show.
Color brightens up our lives
Puts contentment in our souls;
The artist's brush, so full and lush,
Shows beauty, serves His goal.

Gaze at the serpentine of hues
As evening's twilight fades,
Or the purple fist of mountain mist
That levitates for days.
Let senses ride at oceanside
When waves crash to the shore,
Or with moonlight's cast on night's repast
Above where seagulls soar.
The sunlight's sleeves through Autumn's leaves;
All gifts from God's own hand,
For seasons wane, then come again
Refreshed at God's command.

Nancy Watson Dodrill

Summer

The beauty of Summer scenes –
Silvery beaches, forest greens,
Clear blue skies, and rippling streams
Fill my soul with a million dreams.

Summer, with its babbling brooks,
Secluded, cozy little nooks,
Its shading trees, its gentle breeze –
O, Lord, Your wonders never cease.

I could spend endless hours
Looking at the trees and flowers,
All with reverence and sweet prayer
For it's You, Lord, that I see there.

Josephine Anne Miller

Your Word

The Summer sun is shining
And there is fragrance everywhere,
As lovely flowers blossom
And their perfume fills the air.

Lord, Your world is beautiful,
And I thank You everyday
For love and joy and beauty
As I go along my way.

My eyes are wide in wonderment
At all the beauty I see,
That makes all of Your constant love
Oh so real to me.

Dona M. Maroney

For the Lord's word is true; all
His works are trustworthy.
Psalm 33:4

When Faith Is Put Into Action

When we put faith into action,
How quickly we will see
The evidence of things unseen
And God's reality.
We can never walk on water
If we won't leave the boat.
If we're paralyzed by fear,
We may not even float!

When faith is put into action,
Our doubts and fears take wings,
And God gives us the confidence
To try and do all things.
It pleases Him to see us there
When others run away,
To prove that "In God We Trust,"
Reflects our faith today.
When faith is put into action,
Results are guaranteed,
For we're never disappointed
When we follow His lead.
When we put faith into action,
How quickly we will see
The evidence of things unseen
And God's reality!

Clay Harrison

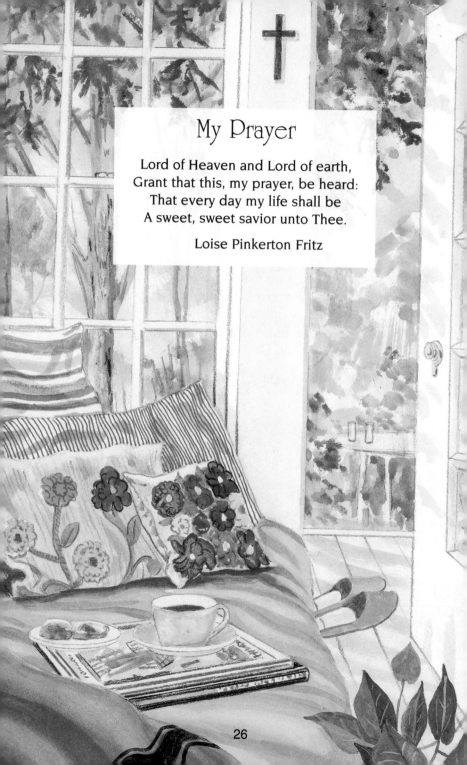

My Prayer

Lord of Heaven and Lord of earth,
Grant that this, my prayer, be heard:
That every day my life shall be
A sweet, sweet savior unto Thee.

Loise Pinkerton Fritz

I'm Sure God Knew...

I'm sure God knew that we would need
A reassuring touch
When He made the friendly handclasp
That warms our hearts so much.
I'm sure He knew that skies of blue
Would ofttime turn to gray;
He put the sunshine in a smile
To chase the clouds away.
God knew, I'm sure, that you and I
Would need a helping hand,
Or a kind word, to let us know
Others care and understand.
God must have known our hearts would need
A special kind of cheer;
I'm sure that's why He sent dear friends
To journey with us here.

Kay Hoffman

*...and live in love, as Christ loved
us and handed Himself over for
us as a sacrificial offering to
God for a fragrant aroma.*
Ephesians 5:2

27

Prayer

It can be said, "Where bended knee
Has touched the barren ground
While praise and reverence pour forth,
His gentle peace is found."
Adding yet, "Our quiet time
Affords unmeasured grace;
It's there the soul surrenders and
Acknowledges His embrace."
Another thing, "More things are wrought
By earnest, simple prayer
Than man could by his strength achieve,
Or by his courage dare."

More can be said, "Our prayer transcends
All circumstance and time,
When one believes, in faith to ask,
In Jesus' name divine!"
So let us now before Him bow
In strengthened faith to claim
The shelter of His promises
As we ask in His name.

Anna Lee Edwards McAlpin

*My strength and my courage is the Lord, and He
has been my Savior. He is my God, I praise Him;
the God of my Father, I extol Him.*
Exodus 15:2

Prayer Will Help

The clatter and confusion
Of a city's daily life
Fills the air with stifling madness
And the heart and mind with strife.
But there is a haven waiting
If we put aside our care;
In the midst of all this turmoil
One need only turn to prayer.
For a whispered plea to Jesus
Will soon calm the tortured soul
Bringing comfort with His blessing
And His help to reach our goal.
Whatever we pursue each day
Should be with all our heart.
Let the obstacles form courage.
Let God lead us from the start.

Helen M. Motti

His Love

The leaves outside my window
Have turned from green to gold,
Reminding me of our Father
And His glory to behold.
He brings the sunshine in the springtime,
Flowers and skies of blue,
Reminding us of His love for me and you.
Come let us adore Him
And show our loyalty
To Jesus, Lord and Savior,
And His love that sets us free.

Dona M. Maroney

*He set me free in the
open; He rescued me
because He loves me.*
Psalm 18:20

Jesus Understands

My Savior knows my every need,
He notes the tears that fall;
He knows when sorrow overwhelms,
And heeds my anguished call.

He cares when I am faint of heart,
And hope is almost gone;
He understands my loneliness
As grey clouds hide the dawn.

'Tis then His nearness comforts me
In such a blessed way,
Assuring me He'll share my grief,
And never from me stray.

Within the shelter of His arms
There's refuge from my fears,
As Jesus soothes my broken heart,
And wipes away all tears.

His presence brings sweet peace to me,
His love becomes the light
That penetrates my troubled soul
And lifts the veil of night!

Beverly J. Anderson

Pray to Understand

Not always does God give to you
The things you ask in prayer.
You'll wonder if He's listening,
Does He really care?
But God knows what is best for you
According to His plan.
So, meanwhile, don't be anxious,
Just pray to understand.

Helen Parker

Winter White

Everything is white today –
The world is sparkling clean;
Snowflakes fell throughout the night
And left a frosty sheen.

The trees are lined with silver;
Each branch reflects the light;
Then dances in the morning sun
And glitters pure and bright.

The white goes on forever –
A sea of purest calm;
Last night the storm of ice and snow
Soothed all the world with balm.

Joan Stephen

Happy the man who
meditates on wisdom, and
reflects on knowledge.
Sirach 14:20

Take great care,
however, to love the
Lord, your God.
Joshua 23:11

36

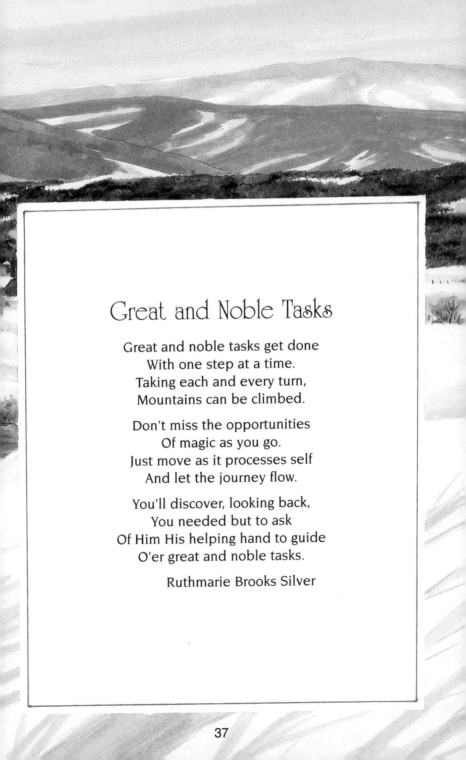

Great and Noble Tasks

Great and noble tasks get done
With one step at a time.
Taking each and every turn,
Mountains can be climbed.

Don't miss the opportunities
Of magic as you go.
Just move as it processes self
And let the journey flow.

You'll discover, looking back,
You needed but to ask
Of Him His helping hand to guide
O'er great and noble tasks.

Ruthmarie Brooks Silver

Each Night and Day

Each night and day I thank dear God above
For His sweet grace and boundless love.
I thank Him for each precious day
Allotted me, and as I pray,
I know that though I've far to go,
He'll stand by me and help me grow
More thoughtful of my fellowman,
Sharing His love as best I can.
And as I drift off into sleep,
He whispers that my soul He'll keep.

Vi B. Chevalier

Our Father Knows
What's Best

Whenever life just seems unfair,
And things don't go your way,
Don't choose to shout and stomp about,
Instead, begin to pray.
For our Father always wants to hear
All things we care about,
Each trial and temptation,
Each worry and each doubt.
When you talk to Him for a little while,
You'll find hope and peace and rest,
And you'll realize, tho' life seems hard,
Our Father knows what's best.

Connie J. Kirby

*You listen, Lord, to the needs of
the poor; You encourage them
and hear their prayers.*
Psalm 10:17

Send Me

So many hurting people, Lord,
Who live within our world –
Who will go and comfort them
As their grief unfurls?

So many, too, who've never heard
The blessed Gospel news:
Who will bring the Word to them?
They have so much to lose!

And what about the old and lonely
Who've shut themselves away –
Thinking no one cares to hear
What they have to say?

Lord, who will go and just visit –
Reach out and touch their hands?
Does no one care? Has it come to that?
No love left in this land?

But suddenly, with pain of heart,
I know that I'm amiss –
I'm quick to point out many faults
While my own I dismiss.

Lord, forgive me for judging others –
So blind I could not see
That I should have said long ago,
"Lord, here I am… send me."

Denise A. DeWald

Holy Spirit

I cannot see the Holy Spirit
But I know that He is there;
I can feel His guiding presence
When I kneel to God in prayer.

And when the choir is singing
And I hear the organ play,
I can feel Him gently touch me –
As He guides me every day.

Luther Elvis Albright

Whispering Heart

My heart whispers a solemn prayer
For all who've lost their way;
May they find a different path
And seek God's love each day.

May my prayers provide a bridge
Between the dark and light,
And in their hearts always walk
Most humbly in His sight.

They've found a special closeness
From which they'll never part,
And ever after listen to
The whispers of the heart.

Angie Monnens

Look to Your Heart

If you feel you have nothing
Of value to give
During these difficult
Times that you live…

Don't surrender your spirit
Because if you do,
You'll forfeit contentment
Allotted to you…

Contentment comes
When you know at the start
You're enriching your soul
As you give of the heart.

Somebody is waiting
For someone like you
To brighten their day
Through a kind deed or two.

It need cost you nothing
In dollars and cents,
Yet think of the rare gift
You'll humbly present.

And only God knows
The graces you'll gain,
While a deep sense of giving
In your heart shall remain.

Catherine Janssen Irwin

Solutions

When we have a problem
The solution is at hand,
We can take it to the Master
For He'll always understand…
The answer may be different
Than what we've planned or sought,
But in God's great wisdom
Some lessons have been wrought…
So we'll keep on praying,
Asking guidance on the way,
Knowing God will lead us
To solutions right each day.

Virginia Borman Grimmer

The Vigil

When I awake I take the time
To meditate and pray,
And call upon Your love to help
Sustain me through the day.
I come to You with tarnished soul
And a mind to do Your will,
But need someone to show me how
This wish I might fulfill.

As the shepherd of Your flock
You keep a watchful eye,
And fill our lives with blessings
On which we must rely.
I long to stay within Your flock,
To be Your little lamb;
Let me be a part of You…
And love me as I am.

Angie Monnens

Song of the Meadow

Strolling through a verdant meadow,
I hear music within my soul.
The ripple of the waltzing grass
Sings to me and makes me feel whole.

Foxtail barley and Queen Anne's Lace
Sway in rhythm with the wind.
My heart is in tune with the music
Where the voices of the meadow blend.

A bluebird rests on a barbwire fence,
Then offers its soprano song.
The chirping staccato of a chickadee
Adds rhythm and tempo to Nature's throng.

The strident voice of a raucous jay
Is just a bit off-key,
But the melding tunes of the meadow
Sound perfectly right to me.

The meadowlark comes to join the chorus,
His happy song adds harmony.
When I listen with a joyful heart –
Nature sings her songs for me.

Charles Clevenger

*May the God of endurance and
encouragement grant you to think
in harmony with one another, in
keeping with Christ Jesus.*
Romans 15:5

49

My Choice

"Have a good day," we often hear
Sometimes in a cheery voice;
My answer is, "Thank you, I will,
You see, it's my God-given choice."
God gave us minds with which to think,
To analyze and choose…
His guidance and His wisdom, too,
Are there for us to use.

Anna M. Matthews

A Simple Prayer

Oh Lord, what simple
Prayers we pray,
Giving You thanks
And glory every day.
Our prayers like misty
Clouds ascend,
Seeking Your wisdom
At each day's end.
May our prayers be worthy
In Your precious sight
As we struggle daily
To do what is right.
May we never
Give into deep despair
As You hear, oh Lord,
Our simple prayer.

Shirley Hile Powell

Nature Testifies

The flowers of the valley and
The lofty trees so grand
Were made by Him who lives on high
To decorate our land.

The setting sun, with golden beams,
Doth gild the heavens so
At eventide when work is o'er
And gentle breezes blow.

The rugged mountains touch the sky,
The broad, deep ocean's foam:
Each in its way tell me that God
Is still upon His throne.

Birds caroling from branches of
The trees resound the theme
That He who made the world still lives
And is fore'er supreme.

Friends, God is love. It's written on
Each spire of grass that grows;
Indelibly it's stamped upon
The petals of each rose.

All things in Nature testify
That God is love and He
Desires us to be happy now
And for eternity.

Luther Elvis Albright

Just Listen

Just listen with a loving heart
To a sister or a brother;
It's a gift to give to someone
So unlike any other.

In a world that can be lonely,
It lets them know you care
About the things within their lives
That they may wish to share.

It tells them that you have the time
To simply be a part
Of life with them and offer up
A kind and loving heart.

Lola Neff Merritt

His Ever-Present Love

Through all the ups and downs of life,
The dark days and the fair,
It's always such a comfort
To know my Lord is there.

To guide and give that needed push
Through life's roughest spots,
When I know that by myself
A winner I am not.

He knows when I'm most likely
To give into despair,
And through His sweet compassion
Hears my silent prayer.

Catherine Janssen Irwin

55

Reflection by the Sea

My God is my companion here,
As I walk the sandy shore –
Reflecting on His righteousness,
Which will last forever more.
I feel the cool and vibrant air
Caress my burning face,
And smell the salty ocean breeze,
Which draws me to this place.
A gentle mist is rising, now,
And with it, lifts my heart –
From burdens that encompassed me,
I feel them all depart.

My mind is filled with quietness,
For peace has been restored –
My heart has been renewed, again,
In the presence of the Lord.
Now, the sun is dipping slowly
Into the shiny sea.
The sky grows orange, then golden –
An awesome thing to see.
As I watch it ever changing,
Then quickly fade away –
I bow my head in gratitude
And thank Him for this day.

Anita G. Hamill

Seeing God

God's love is in the wilderness
And upon the mountains high;
He cares about the sparrow,
He sees the eagle fly.
He leads beside still waters,
We can rest in pastures green;
He gives us strength, and loves us,
His compassion, joy, serene.
We can rest upon His mercy,
We can trust His love and grace;
He surrounds us with strength and power,
His abiding presence, trace.

Norma Woodbridge

An Evening Prayer

Lord... Once again it's time to rest,
I thank You for this day.
Touch me now with quiet grace,
And wash my sins away.
Father... As I put my tasks aside
'Til morning's early light,
Give me strength to see them through,
And wisdom to do them right.
Jesus... Stay beside me through the night,
Your loving vigil keep,
That I may wake to a new day bright,
Refreshed from blessed sleep.
God... Let my body be renewed,
My mind released from care,
My hands at rest from daily toil
And in my heart this evening prayer.

Evy Reis

An Attitude of Love

Life presents us with challenges
That we must overcome,
And sometimes all the detours
Can leave the senses numb.
Life is filled with stumbling blocks
We pass along the way,
But it can become a stepping stone
When love comes into play.

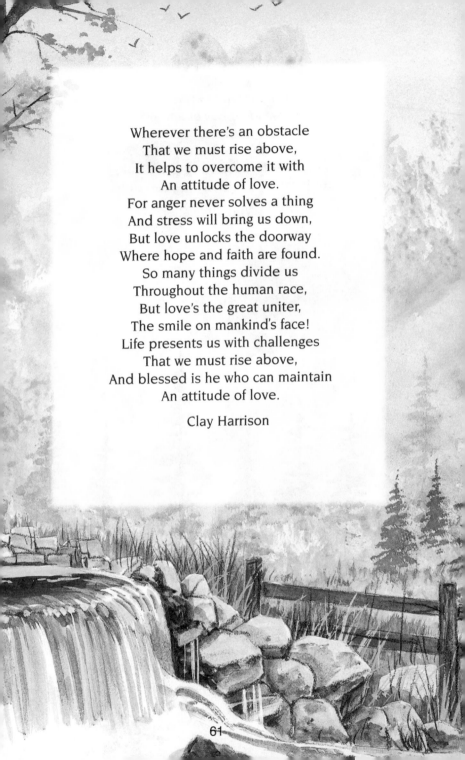

Wherever there's an obstacle
That we must rise above,
It helps to overcome it with
An attitude of love.
For anger never solves a thing
And stress will bring us down,
But love unlocks the doorway
Where hope and faith are found.
So many things divide us
Throughout the human race,
But love's the great uniter,
The smile on mankind's face!
Life presents us with challenges
That we must rise above,
And blessed is he who can maintain
An attitude of love.

Clay Harrison

This I Know

I look around this world and see
God's awesome power and majesty,
And deep within my soul I know
Forevermore it shall be so,
For God is great, His grace divine,
He loves us all through endless time.

Vi B. Chevalier

One Day,
One Thing at a Time

We can't make life go faster
Than just one day at a time,
So why hasten tomorrow,
And leave today's joy behind?
We can't relive yesterday,
So why long for days gone past?
What's taken for granted now
Becomes nostalgic too fast.
One day, one thing at a time,
With the Lord's help, we should live;
Life's sweet hopes and memories
To us He will surely give.

Steven Michael Schumacher

Nothing Is Too Difficult

When I am in despair
And cares weigh heavy on my mind,
And my problems overwhelm me,
Their solutions I can't find;
When it all seems so impossible
The way I just can't see,
A song springs from my spirit –
"Nothing's too difficult for Thee."
It is then I am reminded
Of God's awesomeness and power,
How He formed the hills and mountains
And made each and every flower;
How He makes the sun both rise and set
And causes birds to fly,
And puts the sparkles in the stars,
All this for you and I.

It's when I stop and think of these
And sing my spirit's song,
I know that there is hope
And I will surely get along.
For my troubles and despair are small
Compared to feats as these
And they are not too difficult
For One as such as He.
No, there's nothing that's too difficult
That God can't surely do;
In your times of care and great despair
It's God who'll see you through.

Gina Mazzullo Laurin

Autumn's Showtime

There's a rustling in the walking
And a spryness in the step
At this turning of the seasons,
When the leaves are gold and red.
There's a crispness in the airwaves
And an apple butter scent,
Since Autumn flaunts its beauty
Now that Summer days are spent.

There's a mellowness pervading
That was absent days ago,
And a shriller note is sounded
In the calling of the crow.
The golden moon's more golden,
And the pumpkin's orange glows.
Autumn's curtain has been opened;
Autumn's putting on its show.

Loise Pinkerton Fritz

They speak of the splendor of
Your majestic glory, tell of
Your wonderful deeds.
Psalm 145:5

Does Jesus Cry for Me?

Jesus walked upon this earth
And shared His Father's will;
His gentle Spirit came to love,
His Spirit loves us still.
He cried the tears of heartache
For who wouldn't see…
I wonder if He's crying now
And are those tears for me?

I know how much I've hurt Him
In things I've said and done –
The selfish ways I've lived my life,
The songs I've left unsung.
Dear Lord, will You forgive me
And let me start anew?
Prepare my heart and let me see
What You would have me do.
My hands are Yours for molding,
My feet are Yours to send.
Let me walk beside You now
And be Your earthly friend.
The journey is before us –
I know what I must do.
I'll give my life to hear You say,
"Well done, I'm proud of you."

Jill Lemming

*Build up, build up, prepare the
way, remove the stumbling
blocks from my people's path.*
Isaiah 57:14

Smile

Cheerful is as cheerful does –
Big smiles are all the rage,
So, don't be shy, come on and try
Go twinkle, center stage!
Giggle, laugh and carry on –
See what "Good Will" can do.
The world will be a brighter place
Because of cheerful You…!

Bea Lotz

Fall Foliage

The trees around the lake,
Adorned in shades of Fall,
In crimson, rust and yellow,
Standing so straight and tall.
Adorned in the colors of Autumn,
Reflecting all of their glory,
Shining down into the lake,
Telling Mother Nature's story.
And further on along the road
Were trees still dressed in green,
Refusing to be hurried,
In Autumn colors to be seen.
The landscape was breathtaking,
Spreading out over the land,
The work of a Master Artist
With a very loving hand.

Erna Gwillim

*Adorn yourself with
grandeur and majesty,
and array yourself with
glory and splendor.*
Job 40:10

71

Lord of the Harvest

Lord of the harvest, God of love,
We praise Your holy name.
You send us blessings from above
And treat us all the same.
Your blessings are so many, Lord,
We cannot count them all,
So we bow our heads before You
As night begins to fall.
Lord of the harvest, God of love,
Draw near to us, we pray.
Grant us Thy peace throughout the night
And joy for the coming day.

Grant us courage where there's danger,
Hope where there is doubt,
And the wisdom of Solomon
To work our problems out.
Lord of the harvest, God of love,
May all we say and do
Reflect Thy love within us
And bring honor to You.
May we learn to live in peace, Lord,
As You would have us do,
As we learn to love our brother
And build a bridge to You!

Clay Harrison

Show us, Lord, Your love;
grant us Your salvation.
Psalm 85:8

Through the Night

So often I was weary,
Couldn't sleep all through the night.
I would toss and turn in bed
Until the morning light.

All my thoughts were mingled
With some burdens of the past...
Dwelling on so many things.
I prayed it would not last.

But, suddenly I realized
God sustains me through each plight.
I relaxed, with faith and trust,
And slept all through the night.

Edna Massimilla

A Thanksgiving Prayer

We thank You, Lord, for many things,
Like golden days and birds on wing,
And harvest's wealth before the snow,
And festive meals by candle glow.
We thank You for our loved ones dear
And all our friends who gather here,
Much as the Pilgrims did of yore
To thank You for the Winter's store.
And always we should thank You, too,
For hope that's ever born anew,
That all mankind will comprehend
The way of living You intend,
So that everything we say and do
Reflects the glory that is You.

Mildred M. Marshall

Borrowed Time

The hands of time are turning
Without attaining rest.
To ever-present changes
All Nature can attest.
Season rushes season,
What bloomed just yesterday,
Brings forth fruit for the harvest;
Time moves without delay.
No man can change God's precepts,
Nor make the time stand still.
We all must follow schedules,
Have duties to fulfill.

We work and rest, we win and lose,
Our days are hastening by.
Oh, how we love the joyful hours
Without a tear or sigh.
And someday, looking back on life,
On joys, on grief, and pain,
We wish we could begin anew
And live life over again.

Regina Wiencek

*Lead us back to You, O Lord, that
we may be restored: give us anew
such days as we had of old.*
Lamentations 5:21

Once I prayed, "Lord, have mercy on me; heal me, I have sinned against You."
Psalm 41:5

New Beginnings

Every day is a fresh new start,
A chance for a new beginning,
To live better than the day before,
A day to keep from sinning.

This day can be a day to spread
God's love and peace around,
To thank Him for a lovely world
Where Nature's gifts abound.

Each day a new experience,
A time to thank and pray,
And to feast upon His mercies
While we make it our best day!

Helen Gleason

*Sing out, O heavens, and rejoice,
O earth, break forth into song,
you mountains. For the Lord
comforts His people and shows
mercy to His afflicted.*
Isaiah 49:13

Tender Mercies

For some things there are no shortcuts,
No easy remedies
When life throws you a curve ball
And brings you to your knees.

Sometimes it seems you just can't win
However hard you try
When your faith is sorely tested
And all you do is cry.

It does no good to gripe, complain,
When you're not up to par
Because true friends will understand
And love us as we are.

We sometimes need a helping hand
Before we see the light,
And just knowing prayers are answered
Will help us through the night.

We're not alone in times like these
Unless we choose to be,
For God won't leave us comfortless
In times of tragedy.

There are angels all around us
To catch us when we fall,
And through His tender mercies
We can rise above it all.

Clay Harrison

The Lullaby

Jesus whispers to me a lullaby
As He sings me fast to sleep.
I hear Him in my dreams
After I pray my soul to keep.

It starts with a low hum
Barely audible to my ears;
A rhythm of the ancients,
I am the only one who hears.

I hear His soft, sweet song
Lulling me to sleep.
I am at rest, I am at peace
Because I know my soul He keeps.

Susie Hutton

All Our Burdens

Sometimes God slows us down a bit
And gives us time to cry;
It's then we sit and wonder
And we ask the question, "Why?"

Sometimes pain and broken spirit...
Seems the order of the day,
Yet we know that deep within our hearts
God loves us anyway.

There's a purpose for our suffering,
And our tears are not in vain,
For they cleanse the windows of our hearts
To help God see our pain.

And not one will go unnoticed;
All our burdens He will share,
And be with us every moment,
If we ask of Him in prayer.

Katherine Smith Matheney

God's Love Is Endless

God's love for us is endless
Like the vastness of the sea,
Or the greatness of His Heaven,
And the strongness of a tree.

Each day when we awaken,
His love's already there;
We see it in the sunshine,
Can feel it with each prayer.

We see it in the springtime,
And when Autumn's all aglow;
His love reflects the beauty,
Of the Winter's fallen snow.

The rainbow in its glory,
Seen across the Summer sky;
The host of God's creation,
All within His watchful eye.

The love of God surrounds us,
It will never let us down;
For as long as life is standing,
God's love will be around.

Frances Culp Wolfe

Now and Forever

Guide me, God, from day to day,
Whatever I do, whatever I say,
Help lift me up whenever I fall,
Help me to find some good in all…
Through darkest nights and sunlit days
Help me rejoice and sing Your praise,
And always, always help me be
Your loving child eternally.

Vi B. Chevalier

To Everything There Is a Season

To everything on earth there is a season,
A time for every purpose under the sun.
From the beginning of life's journey to the finish,
We run the race until our days are done.
There is a time for weeping and for laughter,
A time for mourning and a time to dance.
Every favor, every blessing we're receiving
Is a gift of God; it happens not by chance.
For our God, in never failing mercy,
Watches over us from day to dawning day.
In His hands He holds life's changing seasons
As time continues on without delay.

Regina Wiencek

How great are Your works, Lord! How profound Your purpose!
Psalm 92:6

Time Well Spent

It's time well spent when you share
A cup of tea, a laugh or two
With someone who may be lonely
And whose skies are gray instead of blue.
It's time well spent to offer help
To somebody who may be in need,
For a harvest can quickly multiply
Just by planting a tiny seed.

It's time well spent to simply smile,
Adding cheer to someone's life,
For you never know when you'll need a smile
To uplift amid a bit of strife.
It's time well spent to offer thanks
For blessings which come our way –
To be grateful for each sunrise
And sunset at end of day.
It's time well spent to talk to God
Humbly in heartfelt prayer –
Praising Him for all He's done
And releasing every burden and care.

Linda C. Grazulis

Faith is the realization of what
is hoped for and evidence of
things not seen.
Hebrews 11:1

Shadow

A shadow sometimes falls across
The path of life we take.
It may not be of our own choice;
Decisions we must make.
But You are there refining me,
Stretching out my faith.
Walking there beside me, Lord,
Whatever be my fate.
I journey through that shadow time
Not knowing where I'll end;
But one day soon the sun will shine.
Hold tight to me, my Friend.

Ruthmarie Brooks Silver

*How precious is Your love, O
God! We take refuge in the
shadow of Your wings.*
Psalm 36:8

Flight

These simple words, commonly heard,
Bring hope to those storm-tossed, windblown:
"Birds of a feather flock together,
But an eagle soars alone."

Content to fly a solitary high,
I come by myself to God's throne;
Receiving His peace, the spirit's release,
Where His amazing love is shown.

To hear more clearly, follow more nearly,
I seek man's approval no more;
It's important to trust, by faith I must,
Eager to see what's in store.

Every new day, I learn to obey,
His friendship's my only desire;
It's Jesus and me, for eternity,
By His grace alone, I'll fly higher.

Elaine Hardt

A Gift of Love

I bring to you a gift of love
This day so wondrous fair,
A gift of hope and trust and faith,
A gift of gladness rare.
So little else I have to bring
And yet your heart must see,
How very much this gift of love
Is truly part of me.

I bring to you a treasured smile
That you might ever know,
'Tis only sunshine blossoms forth
And helps a heart to grow,

How can we measure kindliness?
We have no way to tell.
We cannot set a value on
A heart where love doth dwell.

I bring to you a gift of joy
A friendship rich and true,
To have and keep forevermore
So much a part of you;
A gift of dreams, a courage sure,
A faith in God above,
And from my heart this priceless gift,
The cherished gift of love.

Garnett Ann Schultz

In Awe

Sometimes I stand in silence,
Sometimes, in awe, I gasp
At the wonders of creation
Too great for a mind to grasp.

Oh, the mighty and the fragile
God's creative hands have made.
How carefully we should keep them;
What trust on us is laid!

Minnie Boyd Popish

My Friend

Thank you for bringing sunshine
To my gray and gloomy days,
For being there when needed,
And for your caring, loving ways.

Thank you for encouragement
When I was weary and distraught,
For words of consolation,
And for all the joy you brought.

Thank you for all your prayers
That were made in my behalf,
For helping to erase my tears
And to replace them with a laugh.

I can face each new tomorrow,
For I know I can depend…
On God who sent an angel,
And it is you my precious friend.

Patience Allison Hartbauer

This we have as an anchor
of the soul, sure and firm...
Hebrews 6:19

The Anchor of My Soul

Tossed about and often drifting,
Daily stresses take their toll
'Til I'm safely back in harbor
With the Anchor of My Soul.

Needless worries, anxious moments
As I try to take control,
Then I'm once again reminded
He's the Anchor of My Soul.

He can calm the raging waters,
He can make the broken whole.
In His presence I take refuge,
Praise the Anchor of My Soul.

Judith B. Schwab

Each Day Is New

Each day is new so look ahead,
The past you cannot undo;
But you can journey with new hope,
And God will see you through.
Don't fret about lost moments,
The sun will shine once more.
Your life can be far richer
Than it's ever been before.
God's love is free and boundless,
It can ease the hurt inside;
Cast out the fear of failure,
Let Him be your constant guide.

He can steer you to new pathways,
Give you health and make you strong.
You can have the Lord's assurance,
That He forgives mistakes and wrong.
Share the joy you have with others;
Give as God has given you.
He has fitted you for service,
And every day you have is new.

Frances Culp Wolfe

Dear Friend

It's nice to have a friend like you,
Someone who always brings
A special touch of caring
To the ordinary things;
Who sees beneath the surface
To the workings of the heart,
Can meet with truth and counterfeit
And tell the two apart.

However many years we live,
We never do outgrow
A need for friends to light the way
Each one of us must go.
No one knows all the answers,
Or where the pathway leads,
But faithful friends have always been...
What everybody needs.

Grace E. Easley

A Merciful God

You have an ocean of mercy,
Mercy for us, O Lord;
You're ne'er depleted of mercy,
There's always more and more.
To thousands of all who love You
And Your commandments keep,
You show to each Your mercy…
A merciful God, indeed.
Though we might stray from Your pathway,
Us, You will never forsake;
You will abundantly pardon,
To mercy You're the gate.
New are Your mercies each morning,
Mercy we need anew;
We will rejoice and be thankful
For mercies shown by You.

Loise Pinkerton Fritz

*…bestowing mercy
down to the thousandth
generation, on the
children of those who
love Me and keep My
commandments.*
Exodus 20:6

Leave the Future Open

Leave the future open
In case God has a plan,
So you can then say "Yes" to Him.
"Take me as You can
To a place where You would have
Me do what You would do.
Take me there and show me.
I will walk therein with You."
For if we clutter up our lives
With things that we would plan,
And do not leave a place therein
To do what He'd do; then…

We'll find ourselves misguided
And fully "out of sync."
But if we leave some space for Him,
Our minds, through His, can think.
So leave the future open,
Let God enter in;
And you will have a future bright
For He will dwell therein.

Ruthmarie Brooks Silver

Trust in the Lord and do
good that you may dwell in
the land and live secure.
Psalm 37:3

Rivers of Blessings

Rivers of blessings flow through my heart
Like those which flow to the sea;
They spring eternal in my breast
And reach to the depths of me.
Rivers of blessings! Rivers of blessings!
O Lord, my God, my Friend,
How can I ever thank You enough
For the rivers of blessings You send?

Phyllis C. Michael

Forgive Me, Lord

Forgive me, oh Lord, when I stumble,
Forgive me for going astray.
I know I'm a weak human being,
And I need You each step of the way.

Sometimes, when I think I'm perfect,
And I feel I can "go it alone,"
You cause me to stop and remember,
That You are still on the throne.

Lord, there are times when I'm helpless,
And everything seems to go wrong.
I call out to You for assurance,
And You hold me until I am strong.

Help me, dear Lord, to be patient,
When trials come my way.
Help me to learn the true meaning,
Of "Only trust and obey."

Helen Ruth Ashton

Slow Down

Slow down and stop your hurry,
Take your time, for life will wait.
Smell the flowers, hear the birds
Even if it makes you late.

Let your eyes feast on the beauties,
Let God touch you as you stroll.
As you view His great creation
Let His message fill your soul.

Slow down, and take time to listen,
You'll have joy as your reward.
The sky of blue, the sea that glistens
All are miracles of the Lord.

Walk in gratitude and wonder
Finding pleasures ever new.
The blessings of our great Creator
Made for us to daily view.

Slow down, take it not for granted
All this beauty 'round we share.
But know that all of Nature's beauty
Speaks of God's great love and care.

Helen Gleason

For this is the message you have heard from
the beginning: we should love one another.
1 John 3:11

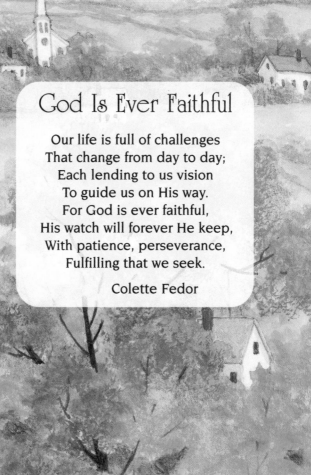

God Is Ever Faithful

Our life is full of challenges
That change from day to day;
Each lending to us vision
To guide us on His way.
For God is ever faithful,
His watch will forever He keep,
With patience, perseverance,
Fulfilling that we seek.

Colette Fedor

Autumn

The sunny hours of yesterday
So recently have flown,
And on their wings they bore away
Some happy days I've known.
At times I've yearned for them again –
Those carefree days gone by,
When laughter floated down the lane
And rarely did I sigh.
Yet now, I taste the ripened grain
That comes from peace within,
Serenity, despite my pain,
A warmth not felt back then.
I gaze outside at falling leaves
All yellow, orange, and red,
And know the joy my Jesus gives –
Life's best is just ahead!

Chris Ahlemann

*Turn Your gaze from me, that
I may find peace before I
depart to be no more.*
Psalm 39:14

God's Love

"Do unto others," says the Golden Rule,
"As you'd have them do unto you."
It's a simple rule to live by,
Day by day – the whole year through.

We all are God's precious children,
No matter the creed, color or race.
Let our lives reflect God's abiding love
So that others will know of His grace.

Don't hide your light 'neath a bushel,
Let it shine – for all to see.
The world is to be our parish
To extend love to humanity.

Have I done my very best, I muse,
Shown charity toward my fellowman;
Have I used my God-given talents
To show God's love where I can?

Don't hide your light in the shadows,
Nor allow it to grow faint or dim.
Let it shine with all its glory –
To proclaim your love for Him.

Charles Clevenger

Thus I will proclaim You,
Lord, among the nations; I will
sing the praises of Your name.
Psalm 18:50

Family Prayer

Springtime and harvest,
Winter and Fall,
Lord, great Provider,
Sustainer of all,
Grant us our portion
Day after day,
May we ever be thankful,
And humble we pray.

Norma Woodbridge

Touch My Brow

Touch my brow, O loving Lord,
Bestow upon me joy!
Let not melancholy ways
Within my heart be stored.
Touch my brow, O Comforter,
Erase the crease found there –
Take my hand and lead me up
On prayer's golden stairs.
Touch my brow, my great Sustainer,
Ignite the spark within!
Till faith has victory once again,
And overcomes my sin.
Touch my brow, O tender Savior,
Remove my inner pain –
Whisper gently through the night
Till only peace remains.

Denise A. DeWald

*At dawn may the Lord bestow
faithful love that I may sing
praise through the night, praise
to the God of my life.*
Psalm 42:9

To Love Unselfishly

Dear Lord, I don't pretend to be
Unselfish, it is true,
For there are many selfish things
So often I will do.

So often I am unconcerned
Or try to judge the way
That someone else is living, Lord,
The things they do each day.

So, Lord, I want to ask You now
To bless the things I do,
And make my heart unselfish, Lord,
To love the way You do.

And help me not to pity self,
But see the world out there
That needs so much more than I do,
So teach me, Lord, to care.

Then teach my heart the meaning of
Concern about another,
To show a kind and loving heart
To all my Christian brothers.

Dear Lord, I know that all of this
Is what You ask of me,
So teach my heart to live and love
Each day unselfishly.

Gertrude B. McClain

Into Your hands I commend my spirit; You will redeem me, Lord, faithful God.
Psalm 31:6

The Holy Spirit

When we open the drapes in the morning,
New light will come pouring in;
We needn't ask nor persuade it to come –
It's just there – as it always has been.
Releasing a sluice after hope for rain,
Clean water will gush through;
We do not beseech – but it will flow,
Refreshing the garden anew.
If we set a wind mill up on a roof,
A breeze will start it to twirl;
The wind doesn't need to be urged to blow
As it sets the sails awhirl.
The Holy Spirit so fills us
Without our request or fanfare,
But as sure as light and water and breeze,
We may know He is always there.

Madolyn Jamieson

*The wind blows where it wills,
and you can hear the sound it
makes, but you do not know
where it comes from or where it
goes; so it is with everyone who
is born of the Spirit.*
John 3:8

119

In the Midst of Your Storm

Do you long for sweet peace
In the midst of your storm?
For a gladness and joy
When your heart has been torn?
Do you long for a calm
In your life filled with grief?
For an enduring strength
When there's doubt in belief?
Yes, I know you do, friend,
For I've been where you are;
And 'tho try as we may
We don't get very far,
Till on Jesus we call
Asking help from above,
Giving Him all our trials,
Trusting His supreme love.

Then He'll give us His grace
That will carry us through;
And He'll strengthen our faith
If we just ask Him to.
As we trust in Him more
There will come a sweet peace
And a comforting calm,
Until our heartaches cease.
If you're weary, dear friend,
Cast your cares upon Him.
Let Him lighten your load
On your pathway grown dim.
How you'll praise Him one day
For the sorrows He's borne
When He came unto you
In the midst of your storm.

Beverly J. Anderson

God's Undying Love

Whenever you are sick and discouraged
And everything seems to go wrong,
Put your hand in the hand of the Savior,
The hands that are loving, but strong.
He promised us "strength for the weary,"
He promised His undying love.
So, if you think You can't take it anymore –
Turn your eyes to the Father above.

Helen Ruth Ashton

My safety and glory are
with God, my strong
rock and refuge.
Psalm 62:8

Reverie

As I gaze over Winter's snow-flecked fields,
Under evening's soft, dove-gray skies;
I can feel sweet peace quietly blanket the land,
Where in Summer bright songbirds fly.

I can feel Winter's hushed, gentle beauty
As I watch in the day's waning light;
And I know God is there in His Heaven
Arranging the stars for night.

Lola Neff Merritt

One thing I ask of the Lord; this I
seek: To dwell in the Lord's house all
the days of my life, to gaze on the
Lord's beauty, to visit His temple.
Psalm 27:4

God's Gift of Life

God gave to us a wonderful gift;
A gift of life and love to share.
We are to follow His example,
Help others feel that life is fair.
At times our life is full of trouble,
Problems surround on every side.
But we cannot give in to sorrow,
Nor should we run away and hide.
We need to offer back to Jesus,
The gift of love He gave to us.
We ought to serve Him with passion;
Let others know in Him we trust.
We need to bear another's burden:
Walk with them on their road of life,
Encourage them to higher values,
Help them to conquer fear and strife.
The inner strength God will give us,
Will help us face life with a smile.
In valleys low or on the mountain,
He'll make our road of life worthwhile.

Frances Culp Wolfe

May the God of hope fill you with all joy and peace in believing, so that you may abound in hope by the power of the Holy Spirit.

Romans 15:13

Still There Is Hope

Cold winds blow merciless across my brow,
Life seemed better yesterday, somehow;
Happiness has flown with swallow's swift,
Through ashes of my broken dreams I sift.
Still there is hope that mounts on fairer wings,
Sweet peace is mine, the aching heart still sings;
This, too, will pass, this valley dark and lone,
A still, small voice is beckoning, follow on.
There comes another dream, set expectations high,
Believe in the impossible, God hears your cry,
And with the newborn day allow new hope to rise;
By faith stay on the path that veiled before you lies.

Regina Wiencek

May Your kindness, Lord, be upon
us; we have put our hope in You.
Psalm 33:22

My people will
live in peaceful
country, in secure
dwellings and
quiet resting
places.
Isaiah 32:18